Welcome to  xtb and Table Talk

Exploring the Bible together to discover God's Rescue Plan

XTB stands for **EXplore The Bible**.

Read a bit of the Bible each day.
Unscramble the meaning of Easter with the help of Dr. Luke.
Find out all about God's Rescue Plan.

Are you ready to explore the Bible? Fill in the bookmark...
...then turn over the page to start exploring with XTB!

C000225523

Table Talk FOR FAMILIES

Table Talk helps children and adults explore the Bible together. It can used by:

- Families
- One adult with one child
- Children's leaders with their groups
- Any other way you want to try

Table Talk uses the same Bible passages as XTB so that they can be used together if wanted. Table Talk is enclosed at the back of this book. It's easy to spot because it's printed sideways

Never done anything like this before? Check our web page for some further help (www.thegoodbook.co.uk/daily_reading/xtb.htm) or write in for a fact sheet.

....

.... **(nickname)**

My birthday is

....

My age is

....

I like Easter because

....

How to find your way around the Bible...

Look out for the **READ** sign.
It tells you what Bible bit to read.

**READ
Luke 19v10**

So, if the notes say... **READ Luke 19v10**
...this means chapter 19 and verse 10
...and this is how you find it.

Use the **Contents** page in your Bible to
find where Luke begins

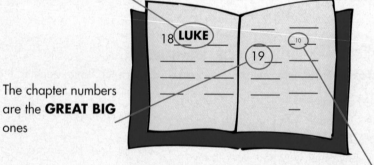

18 LUKE   19   10

The chapter numbers
are the **GREAT BIG**
ones

The verse numbers are the
tiny ones!

Oops! Keep getting lost?
Cut out this bookmark and use it to keep your place.

How to use

 1 Find a time and place when you can read the Bible each day.

 **2** Get your Bible, a pencil and your XTB notes.

 **3** Ask God to help you to understand what you read.

 **4** Read today's XTB page and Bible bit.

 **5** Pray about what you have read and learnt.

 **6** If you can, talk to an adult about what you've learnt. Remind them about **Table Talk** at the back of this booklet

Rescue! stickers

This Easter pack comes with free **Rescue!** stickers. Be ready to stick one in every time Luke tells us something about God's Rescue Plan.

(If your stickers are missing, contact us at the address inside the front cover and we'll send you some more.)

Are you ready to find out about **God's Rescue Plan?** Stick your first sticker here, then hurry on to Day 1.

DAY 1 EASTER EGGSTRAVAGANZA!

Luke 19v10

What is Easter all about? Bunnies, hot cross buns and chocolate? *Crack the egg code and see!*

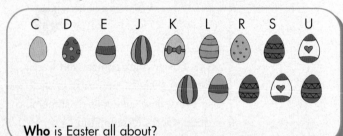

C D E J K L R S U

Who is Easter all about? _ _ _ _ _ _

Read today's Bible verse to see what Jesus said about why He came. (*By the way, when Jesus says "**Son of Man**", He is talking about **Himself**.*)

READ
Luke 19v10

Jesus said that He "came to look for and S_____ the lost."

Easter is about being _ _ _ _ _ _

Stick a Rescue! sticker here ➡️

God's Rescue Plan
The first part of the Bible (the Old Testament) shows that people are in trouble. They need to be rescued. God promised that He would send a **Rescuer** (Saviour), called the Messiah or Christ.

We're going to find out about God's Rescue Plan from one of the books in the New Testament.

Who wrote it? _ _ _ _ _ _

Dr. Luke wrote his book (called Luke's Gospel) to show **WHO** the Rescuer is and **WHY** we need rescuing. Luke shows us that **Jesus** is the promised Rescuer. (*You can discover more about Luke on the back page of this book.*)

PRAY
Dear God, please help me to learn more about your Rescue Plan as I read Luke's book. *Amen*

DAY 2 DONKEY RIDING

The first Easter week starts with some unexpected transport, and a lot of shouting!

READ
Luke 19v28-31

How did Jesus travel into Jerusalem? By C_____

 car?   colt?   camel?   caravan?

DID YOU KNOW?

500 years earlier, an Old Testament writer called Zechariah had said that God's chosen **KING**—who had come to **RESCUE** His people—would ride into Jerusalem on a colt: that's a young donkey.
(*You can read this promise for yourself in Zechariah 9v9*)

When people saw Jesus riding into Jerusalem on a donkey they got really excited…

What were the people shouting?

READ
Luke 19v35-40

God bless the K_____ who comes in the name of the L_____! (v38)

The religious leaders wanted the people to stop shouting.
But what did Jesus say would happen if they stopped? (v40)

xtb   Luke 19v28-40

Imagine that the stones really did start to shout! *What do you think they might have said?*

Jesus the King has come to rescue His people—and it's so important that even rocks will yell about it!

THINK + PRAY

The people praised God for sending Jesus. What do you want to praise and thank God for?

DAY 3 CLEAR OFF!

xtb Luke 19v45-48

Spot 10 coins hidden in the picture

Read the Bible verses to find out what's happening.

What had God said His Temple should be called?

A **H**_____ of **P**_____ (v46)

BUT!!!
The Temple courtyard was full of lying salesmen. The people who came to pray to God were **cheated** out of their money!

So what did Jesus do?(v45)

READ
Luke 19v45-46

READ
Luke 19v47-48

The religious leaders **hated** what Jesus did and said. They wanted to get rid of Him as soon as possible.

More about their secret plans tomorrow.

Sometimes we see things happening that we know are wrong.

For example, a new boy has joined Dave's school but nobody will talk to him. *As a follower of Jesus what should Dave do?*

What would **you** do?

PRAY
Ask God to help you to act the way He wants you to—even when that's difficult or could make you unpopular.

DAY 4 THE PLOT THICKENS

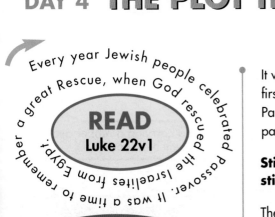

Every year Jewish people celebrated a great Rescue, when God rescued the Israelites from Egypt. It was a time to remember

READ
Luke 22v1

Cross out every x, y + z

What was **Passover** about?
(*the spiral gives a clue*)

XRYZEXYSZXCYUZXEY

What is **Easter** about?

ZYRXEZYSXZCYUXZEY

It wasn't by accident that the first Easter happened at Passover time. It was all part of God's Rescue Plan.

Stick a Rescue! sticker here

There were **two plans** happening at the same time.
1. God's Rescue Plan
2. The Murder Plot!

READ
Luke 22v2-6

THE MURDER PLOT
Jesus' enemies wanted to get rid of Him. They were trying to find a way to have Him murdered secretly. One of Jesus' disciples agreed to help.

Who was he?(v4) **J** _____

GOD'S RESCUE PLAN
Amazingly it had always been part of God's Rescue Plan that Jesus would die. **Not** so that His enemies could get rid of Him, but so that Jesus could **rescue** His people.

As we carry on reading Dr. Luke's book we will see both plans in action. Sometimes it may **look** like the wicked murder plot is winning—but Luke will show us that God is **always** in control.

PRAY

Dear God, thank you that you are always in charge. Please help me to trust You.

DAY 5 FOLLOW THAT JAR!

1

READ
Luke 22v7-13

What are Peter and John doing? Read the Bible passage to find out.

2

Correct the mistakes in these instructions.

Go and get breakfast ready. (v8)

 A girl carrying a rubber duck will meet you. (v10)

Don't follow anybody! (v10)

Get the garden ready for our barbecue. (v12)

JESUS IS IN CHARGE

3

Jesus' friends knew that the Passover meal was a time to remember a great Rescue—but they didn't know that it was also part of a **much greater rescue**—God's Rescue Plan for the whole world!

Did you know?

The first ever Passover meal happened when God rescued Moses and the Israelites from slavery in Egypt. *If you want to know more read Exodus 12v1-14*

4

- Jesus knew this would be His last meal with His friends.
- He knew all about the murder plot too!
- Jesus knew **everything** that would happen—He was always in control.

THINK + PRAY

Jesus knows **everything** that happens to you. How does that make you feel? **Talk to God about it.**

DAY 6 — READY TO REMEMBER

Put a tick (✔) by the foods you like best.

Now (circle) the foods you think Jesus may have eaten with His friends at Passover.
(*Answers at the bottom of the page.*)

Jesus knew He was going to die, and wanted to help His friends to be ready.

READ
Luke 22v14-20

Follow the lines to see what each thing reminds us of.

Passover — Jesus' blood (v20)
Bread — Rescue from Egypt
Wine — Jesus' body (v19)
Easter — God's Rescue Plan

Jesus wanted His friends to understand that **this Rescue** is far more important than that first rescue from Egypt. **This is the one to remember**.

Did you know?

Christians eat bread and drink wine to remind them that Jesus died to rescue them. In different chuches, this may be called Communion, Breaking of Bread, Eucharist or the Lord's Supper.

In **XTB** we use the Rescue! stickers to help us to remember God's Rescue Plan. *Stick a rescue sticker here.*

RESCUE

What else could you do to remind you of the first Easter?

e.g. draw a picture or...
make hot cross buns or...

If you can, do it now!

PRAY

Dear God, thank you for sending Jesus as the Rescuer. Please help me never to forget that He died for me.

Answer: The Passover meal included bread, wine and roast lamb

DAY 7 TEMPTING TIMES

Your mum tells you to tidy your room. *Do you...*

a) Go and do it straight away
b) Put it off until later
c) Pretend you didn't hear her

Most of us find it hard to do what we're told. We put things off if we can.

In today's reading, Jesus has a choice to make. He knows that a horrible death is waiting for Him. *Will He try to put it off?*

READ
Luke 22v39-46

Did Jesus find it easy to obey God?
Yes / No
(Check v42-44 if you're not sure)

Jesus needed God's help. Who did God send to strengthen Jesus? (v43)

_____

How did Jesus end His prayer?

Not m____ will, but y_____ will be done. (v42)

Jesus chose to obey God, even though it would be very hard.

When Jesus had finished praying, He went back to the disciples. What were they doing? (v45) *Tick your answer*

eating   sleeping

praying

Jesus had a **choice**. He chose to obey God.

The disciples had a **choice**. They fell asleep!

THINK + PRAY

Living the way God wants us to **isn't** easy. It makes no difference what age you are, or how long you've been a friend of Jesus. We **all** need God's help.

Think of a time this week when you might find it hard to obey God.
(*At home? At school? With your friends?*)
Ask God to help you to obey Him like Jesus did.

Imagine the scene. It's dark. Night time. The crowd marching down the hill are carrying swords, clubs and torches. Jesus can see them coming. He has plenty of time to escape. *But will He?*

READ
Luke 22v47-48

Who betrayed Jesus? **J**_____

As we zoom in on the action the torchlight glints off the sharp edge of a sword. One of Jesus' followers is fighting back. A swoosh—a yell—and a man is hurt. *What will Jesus do now?*

READ
Luke 22v49-51

Jesus could have escaped—but He didn't! When His friends tried to protect Him, Jesus stopped them. Then He healed the injured man.
Crack the code to find out why.

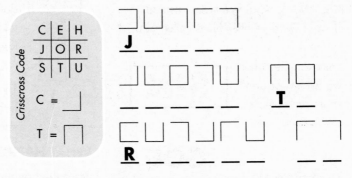

Crisscross Code

C	E	H
J	O	R
S	T	U

C = ⌐

T = ⌐

J _ _ _ _ _ _

_ _ _ _ _ _ _ _ _ _ **T** _

R _ _ _ _ _ _ _ _ _ _

Jesus didn't fight back because He chose to die as our Rescuer. Read **The Sin Solution** on the next page to find out why.

Stick a Rescue! sticker here ➡

PRAY Thank Jesus that He chose to die to rescue you.

THE SIN SOLUTION

We know that Jesus is the Rescuer - but **WHY** do we need rescuing?

WHAT IS SIN?

We all like to be in charge of our own lives. We do what **we** want, instead of what **God** wants. This is called Sin.

For example, when we tell lies or don't share with others.

WHAT DOES SIN DO?

Sin separates us from God. It stops us from knowing Him and stops us being His friends. The final result of sin is death. You can see why we need a Rescuer!

HOW DOES JESUS RESCUE US?

At the first Easter, when Jesus was about 33 years old, He was crucified. He was nailed to a cross and left to die.

As He died all the sins of the world (all the wrongs people had done) were put onto Jesus. He took all of our sin onto Himself, taking the punishment we deserve. He died in our place, as our Rescuer, so that we can be forgiven.

When Jesus died, He dealt with the problem of sin. That means that there is nothing to separate us from God any more. That's great news for you and me! **And there's more...**

WHAT HAPPENED NEXT?

Jesus died on the cross as our Rescuer - but He didn't stay dead! After three days God brought Him back to life. Jesus is still alive today, ruling as King.

Is Jesus your Rescuer, Friend and King? **Turn to the next page to find out...**

AM I A CHRISTIAN?

Not sure if you're a Christian? Then check it out below...

Christians are people who have been rescued by Jesus and follow Him as their King.

You can't become a Christian by trying to be good.

That's great news, since you can't be totally good all the time!

It's about accepting what Jesus did on the cross to rescue you. To do that, you will need to **ABCD**.

A **Admit** your sin—that you do, say and think wrong things. Tell God you are sorry. Ask Him to forgive you, and to help you to change. There will be some wrong things you have to stop doing.

B **Believe** that Jesus died for you, to take the punishment for your sin; that He came back to life, and that He is still alive today.

C **Consider** the cost of living like God's friend from now on, with Him in charge. It won't be easy. Ask God to help you do this.

D **Do** something about it! In the past you've gone your own way rather than God's way. Will you hand control of your life over to Him from now on? If you're ready to ABCD, then talk to God now. This prayer will help you.

> Dear God,
> I have done and said and thought things that are wrong. I am really sorry. Please forgive me. Thank you for sending Jesus to die for me. From now on, please help me to live as one of Your friends, with You in charge.
> **Amen**

If you have prayed this prayer, or one like it, then you are a Christian. You have been rescued by Jesus. That's great!

Lots of speech bubbles today.
But what's it all about?

FLASH BACK—to a few hours earlier... *(from Luke 22v33-34)*

Lord, I am ready to go to prison with you and to die with you!

Peter

I tell you, Peter, the cock will not crow tonight until you have said three times that you do not know me.

Jesus

*Who was right? Peter or Jesus?
Read the verses to find out.*

READ
Luke 22v54-62

Peter said **three times** that he didn't know Jesus.
Put these speech bubbles in the right order. (v57, 58 & 60 will help)

A Man, I don't know what you're talking about!

B Man, I am not!

C Woman, I don't even know him!

1 = ___   2 = ___   3 = ___

When Peter heard the cock crow, he realised that he had lied about knowing Jesus—just as Jesus said he would. *What did Peter do then?(v62)*

THINK SPOT

Peter was sick with himself for lying about Jesus. *How do* **you** *feel when you let Jesus down?*

THINK + PRAY

Think about ways you have let Jesus down this week. Tell Him how you feel, and ask Him to forgive you. *Write your prayer in the speech bubble.*

Dear Jesus, I'm sorry...

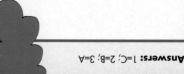

Answers: 1=C; 2=b; 3=A

DAY 10 WHO'S ON TRIAL?

 was caught red-handed. Creeping out of the with the

stolen  under his arm. saw him do it. arrested him.

Now he's on trial, up in front of

Do you think he'll be found guilty or innocent? _____

Just like Sneaky Sam, Jesus was put on trial. The difference is that Jesus had done **nothing** wrong!

READ
Luke 22v66-71

Find three titles for Jesus:

1. The _____ (v67)
2. The Son of M_____ (v69)
3. The Son of G_____ (v70)

WOW!

God had promised to send a new King to rescue His people. These titles meant that Jesus was the one! He had been sent by God as the promised **Rescuer** and **King**.

Time for a Rescue! sticker

But did His enemies believe Jesus was the Rescuer? Yes / No

Jesus enemies **didn't believe** that Jesus was the promised Rescuer. They just wanted to get rid of Him!

THINK SPOT

What do **you** believe about Jesus?
Tick your answers
☐ Jesus is the Son of God
☐ Jesus died to rescue me
☐ Jesus hears me when I pray to Him
☐ Jesus loves me
☐ Jesus wants me to be His friend

PRAY

Dear Jesus, please help me to learn more about you from the Bible, and to believe what it tells me.

THE MURDER PLOT

Jesus' enemies wanted to kill Him. But Israel was part of the Roman empire. Only the **Romans** were allowed to sentence anyone to death. So Jesus was taken to the **Roman Governor**—Pontius Pilate.

READ
Luke 23v1-4

What did Pilate decide about Jesus? *Copy verse 4 into the speech bubble.*

I find...

Pilate knew Jesus was **innocent**!

Pilate wanted to get out of this tricky situation, so he sent Jesus to Herod Antipas, the local ruler of Galilee.

READ
Luke 23v8-11

Herod had wanted to see Jesus for a long time. *Why? (v8)*

He wanted to see Jesus perform _____

Herod **didn't care** who Jesus was—he just wanted to see an exciting miracle!

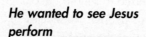
Did you know?

Herod's father—also called Herod!— had tried to have Jesus killed when He was a baby.

GOD'S RESCUE PLAN

These powerful men could have freed Jesus—but they didn't! It *looked* like the murder plot was winning. But as we already know, this was all part of **God's Rescue Plan**. Jesus was going to die to rescue His people.

THINK + PRAY

It makes no difference how powerful someone is. God is **more powerful**—and His plans always come true.

That means that you can always trust God to keep His promises. **Thank** God that He will never let you down.

DAY 12 FREEDOM (BUT FOR WHO?)

It was Passover time. (The spiral on *Day 4 will remind you what Passover is about.*) Every year, the Romans set one prisoner free at Passover. This year, Pilate wanted to free Jesus.

But would the people agree?

READ
Luke 23v18-25

Pilate gave the people **two** choices. They could free a murderer called **Barabbas**, or **Jesus** their King.

Who was set free? (v25)

_____

Who was sentenced to death?_____

These people **all** rejected Jesus.
(*Find them in the wordsearch.*)

PILATE   **HEROD**
PRIESTS   **LEADERS**
PEOPLE   **CROWD**

```
        D  C
        O  R
        R  O
        E  W
        H  D
      E T A L I P
    E V E R Y O N E
      P E O P L E
        P  S
        R  R
        I  E
        E  D
        S  A
        T  E
        S  L
```

What word is left over?

E _ _ _ _ _ _ _ _

The people who voted to have Jesus killed weren't the only ones who rejected Jesus. The Bible says that **everyone** turns their backs on Jesus. We do what **we** want instead of what **He** wants. This is called **Sin**.

Jesus was going to die. Not just for the sins of a <u>few</u> people, but for <u>everyone</u>. That includes the people who voted to have Him killed. It includes **me**. And it includes **you!**

PRAY Thank you Jesus, that You came to rescue everyone, including me!

DAY 13 THE KING WHO CAME TO DIE

 xtb Luke 23v32-38

Crucifixion was used by the Romans as a way to kill criminals. Jesus had done **nothing** wrong—but He was crucified just like a criminal! He was nailed to a cross and left to die. Two other men were put to death at the same time.

READ
Luke 23v32-38

It was a Roman custom to put a **sign** on each cross to show what that person had done wrong. The men hanging on the right and left of Jesus were both **thieves**. What did the sign on **Jesus'** cross say?(v38)

> T _ _ _ is the K _ _ _ of the J _ _ _

*Copy the sign for each man. Remember that Jesus is in the **middle**.*

Use these words:

THIEF
THIEF
KING

Jesus

What did Jesus say when He was nailed to the cross?(v34)

> F _ _ _ _ _ _ _ _
> **them, Father!**

WOW!

The sign on Jesus' cross was right. He <u>was</u> the King. A King who came to **die** so that His people could be forgiven.

THINK + PRAY

Jesus died to forgive people for their sins. Even the people who killed Jesus could be forgiven! Say thank you to God that nothing we do is so bad that we can't be forgiven.

DAY 14 WHO CAN BE SAVED?

Imagine what Jesus looked like on the cross. Bruised. Bleeding. Dying. The sign above His head said "King", but He didn't **look** like a King! As the soldiers watched Jesus dying, they made fun of Him. So did one of the thieves who was hanging next to Jesus.

READ
Luke 23v39-43

One thief threw insults at Jesus. But the other didn't. He knew that Jesus had done nothing wrong. And he **believed** that Jesus was the promised King. *Complete the speech bubbles.* **Use these words:**

Today Remember

King Jesus

Paradise

Why did Jesus make this incredible promise to a dying man? Because Jesus knew His death would **rescue** people from sin. Check out **The Sin Solution** after Day 8 to remind you of what happened.

Which thief went to be in Paradise with Jesus?
The one who **believed** in Jesus or the one who **didn't believe**?

The thief who
_____

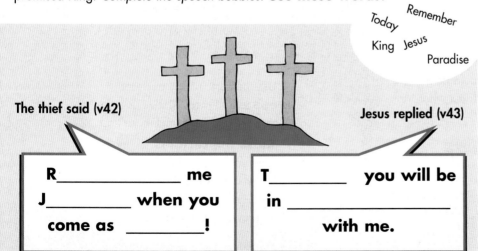

The thief said (v42)

R_____ me
J_____ when you
come as _____!

Jesus replied (v43)

T_____ you will be
in _____
with me.

PRAY Thank you Jesus, that You came to rescue everyone who believes in You.

DAY 15 THE KING IS DEAD

Imagine watching this on TV. A cruel death. Soldiers guarding their victims. Crowds mocking. Friends weeping. It's the middle of the day—but suddenly the sun stops shining! For three hours! It all seems terrible. Surely the wicked murder plot has won.

But this is **NOT** the end! And the clue comes from a curtain...

READ
Luke 23v44-46

This **isn't** a window curtain! This huge curtain separated the rest of the Temple from the bit in the middle—where God was said to live. Only the high priest could go in, and only once a year! Nobody else was allowed. But what happened when Jesus died? (v45)

The curtain was t_____ in two.

This curtain was a picture of what sin does. It reminded people that sin separated them from God.

WOW!

When Jesus died, He dealt with the problem of sin. That's why the curtain in the Temple was ripped in two, to show there is nothing to separate us from God any more.

Jesus died to rescue us from Sin ➡️

THINK + PRAY

Use the curtains in your room to help you to pray. (If it's dark, you may want to wait until morning.)

Close the curtains — think about how your sin separates you from God.
Now open the curtains — and thank God that Jesus died to take away your sin.

THREE REACTIONS

Luke
23v47-49

Jesus had just died. How did people react?

READ
Luke 23v47-49

1 The Roman centurion was in charge of the crucifixion. But when he saw how Jesus died, he **praised** God!
What did he say? (v47)

Note: Being "righteous" (NIV) means being "right with God".

He was a
_____ man

2 The crowds watching were sad at what they saw.
*What did they do to show their **sorrow**? (v48)*

_____

3 As the crowds left, what did Jesus' friends do? (v49)

a) Go home too
b) Watch from a distance
c) Talk to the Roman soldiers

Jesus' friends would still be there to see **what happened next**. *More about that tomorrow.*

THINK SPOT

What about **you**?
How do **you** react to Jesus' death?

A Does it make you **sad**?
Yes / No / Sometimes

Why?

B Does it make you **happy**?
Yes / No / Sometimes

Why?

THINK + PRAY

The day Jesus died is called **Good Friday**. Jesus did a **good** thing when He rescued us from our sin. **Thank God for sending Jesus to rescue you.**

DEAD AND BURIED

READ
Luke 23v50-56

Who buried Jesus' body? (v50)

J_____

(from Arimathea)

Who did Joseph ask first? (v52)

P_____

Who was watching? (v55)

Some **W**_____

These people all knew for sure that Jesus was dead. But they had no idea what would happen next!

What was the body wrapped in?

_____(v53)

Did you know?

The tomb was like a cave, cut out of solid rock. It was sealed up with a huge stone.

If you know the end of the story, you'll know that there is a wonderful surprise coming up! But Jesus' friends **didn't** know that yet...

Actually, Jesus had told them what would happen to Him—but they didn't understand.

If you have time, read Jesus' promise to His followers in **Luke 18v31-34.**

THINK + PRAY

Like Jesus' friends, we sometimes find it hard to understand what God is telling us in the Bible, or to believe that He will do what He says. Ask Him to help you to understand and believe His promises.

DAY 18 — HE IS NOT HERE...

xtb — Luke 24v1-12

Start today's page by cracking the arrow code.

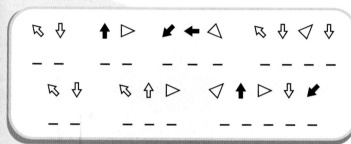

↘ ⇓ ↑ ▷ ↙ ← ◁ ↘ ⇓ ◁ ⇓

_ _ _ _ _ _ _ _ _ _ _

↘ ⇓ ↘ ⇧ ▷ ◁ ↑ ▷ ⇓ ↙

_ _ _ _ _ _ _ _ _ _

Read today's verses to see who said this and why.

Arrow Code

A = ⇧
E = ⇓
H = ↘
I = ↑
N = ↙
O = ←
R = ◁
S = ▷
T = ◁

READ
Luke 24v1-9

Did you know?

Risen • Raised • Resurrection
These words all mean a dead person coming back to life.

WOW!

Jesus didn't stay dead! God brought Him back to life again!

Peter went to check for himself.

What did Peter see?
a) Nothing at all
b) The body wrapped in linen cloth
c) The linen cloth—but no body!

READ
Luke 24v10-12

Think about how people reacted. The women were **puzzled** (v4) and **scared** (v5). The disciples **didn't believe** (v11). Peter was **amazed** (v12).

THINK + PRAY

Think about Jesus coming back to life. Are you puzzled, scared, don't believe, amazed or something different?

Talk to God about your answer.

DAY 19 PUZZLING PERAMBULATIONS!*

Jesus was **alive**—but His **friends** didn't know that yet! Two of them walked to a nearby village, called Emmaus. On the way, **Jesus** came and walked with them—but they didn't **recognise** Him! They were sad and **puzzled** by everything that had happened, so Jesus showed them what the **Scriptures** (the oldest part of the Bible) said about Him.

READ
Luke 24v25-27

Fit the underlined words into the crossword.

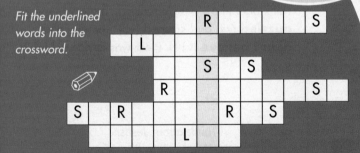

Jesus explained that He died to scue His people.

Stick a Rescue! sticker here

Jesus' followers still didn't know it was Him—but they asked Jesus to have a meal with them.

READ
Luke 24v28-35

At last, the two friends knew it was Jesus! They dashed back to Jerusalem to tell the rest of Jesus' followers that Jesus was alive! Their great news was far too important to keep to themselves.

THINK + PRAY

Who can **you** tell about Jesus this week?

_____

Ask God to help you to tell your friends about Jesus.

* **Perambulating** means **walking**. Use it to impress your teacher or to confuse your dog! ("Heel Fido—Perambulations!")

Magic Marvin can pull a rabbit out of a hat—but you know it's just a clever **trick**.

Jesus' friends found it hard to believe that He really was alive again. They needed to be sure that it **wasn't** just a trick.

READ
Luke 24v36-45

How did Jesus help them?

Fit in the missing verse numbers.

v43 v36 v45 v39

- They **saw** Jesus v___
- They **touched** Jesus v___
- They **ate** with Jesus v___
- They **listened** to Jesus explain everything v___

Which of these would help **you?** *Tick your answers*

Seeing and touching Jesus wasn't enough for Jesus' friends. Verse 41 says that they still didn't believe it. *So what did Jesus do?*
Take the first letter of each picture to find the answer.

— — — — — —   — — — —   — — — —

The Scriptures (the oldest part of the Bible) show God's promise to send a **Rescuer**, who would die to save His people. Jesus helped His friends to understand that **He** was this Rescuer—who died and came back to life again.

THINK + PRAY

Want to know more?
For a free booklet called **Why did Jesus rise?** write to us at XTB, 37 Elm Road, New Malden, Surrey, KT3 3HB Or email: alison@thegoodbook.co.uk

Do you want to know Jesus better, and understand what the Bible says about Him? If so, you need to ask for His help. Ask Jesus to open your mind, so that you come to know Him better and better.

DAY 21 UP, UP AND AWAY!

What's Next for Jesus?

We've reached the end of Luke's book—but it's **not** the end of the story! Read on to see what happens next...

READ
Luke 24v50-53

Dr. Luke tells us more about this story in his next book—**Acts**. *You can read it in Acts 1v6-11*

Did you know?

Jesus is still alive today in heaven. He didn't die again. He is King for ever!

What's Next for the Disciples?

Look again at how Luke ends his book in v52-53 —then fill in the gaps. **Use these words:**

thanks   joy   Temple   Jesus

They worshipped J_____ and went back into Jerusalem, filled with great _____ , and spent all their time in the _____ giving _____ to God.

THINK SPOT

The disciples were full of joy because Jesus was their Rescuer. Are **you**?

What's Next for You?

Well done for reaching the end of Easter Unscrambled! There's still loads more of the Bible to explore. **What Next?** (on the back page) has some ideas to start you off.

And remember—Jesus is still alive today. He will help you to understand the Bible as you read it.

PRAY

Father God, thank you for bringing Jesus back to life. Thank you that He is still alive today and I can talk with Him. Please help me to follow Him always. Amen

WELCOME TO TABLE TALK

The aim of this section is to help you to read the Bible together as a family. Each day provides a short family Bible time which, with your own adaptation, could work for ages 4 to 10. We've included some optional follow on material linked with the XTB children's notes, which take the passage further for 7-10s.

BUILDING UP

The Building Up section of the family pack is designed to link up with XTB children's notes. After your child has worked through XTB on their own, the questions in Building Up can be used to build on what they have learnt. Questions may reinforce the main teaching point, stretch your child's understanding or develop how the passage applies to us today.

Building Up can also be used as an extra question section to add to those in Table Talk. This may be particularly valuable if you have older children.

TABLE TALK

A short family Bible time for daily use. Table Talk takes about five minutes, maybe at breakfast, or after an evening meal. Choose whatever time and place suits you best as a family.

Table Talk includes a simple discussion starter or activity that leads into a short Bible reading. This is followed by a few questions and a suggestion for prayer.

Table Talk can be used on its own, or alongside the XTB children's notes.

xtb XTB Bible reading notes for children are based on the same passages from Luke as Table Talk. XTB notes can be used on their own, or with Table Talk.

Suggestions for using XTB and Table Talk:

★ The family do **Table Talk** together at breakfast. Older children do **XTB** on their own later, then share what they've learnt with a parent using **Building Up.**

★ **Or:** Children use **XTB** notes on their own.

★ **Or:** Children's leaders use **XTB** and **Table Talk** to read the Bible with their group.

★ **Or:** Some or all of the family use **Table Talk** as the basis for a short family time, with added questions from the **Building Up** section when appropriate.

Today's passages are:
Table Talk : Luke 19v10
XTB : Luke 19v10

TABLE TALK

DO

Hunt through the toy box together. What can you find that's about being **RESCUED?** e.g. a police car, nurse's outfit, Fireman Sam book, ambulance... What kind of people rescue us?

READ

Easter is all about being **Rescued**. Read what Jesus said (to a very short man called Zacchaeus) about why He came. **Read Lk 19v10**.

TALK

What name did Jesus call Himself? ("Son of Man"—this title is used in Daniel 7v13-14 to refer to the Messiah (Christ)—Jesus often used it to refer to Himself.) What did Jesus say He came for? (To look for and save lost people.) Easter is all about being rescued, because Jesus came as our **Rescuer**. This is **God's Rescue Plan** for the world.

PRAY

Ask God to help you learn more about His Rescue Plan this Easter.

BUILDING UP

Today's **XTB** notes show that Easter is about being rescued.

Ask your child what Easter is about. Did it surprise them to find that Easter is about being rescued? Why/why not? Ask them to explain the Rescue! stickers to you.

Today's passages are:
Table Talk : Luke 19v36-38
XTB : Luke 19v28-40

TABLE TALK

How many ways could you travel into the middle of town? (Bus, walk, pogo-stick...) When Jesus arrived in Jerusalem, He rode in on a young donkey.

READ

(Optional!) **Look up Zechariah 9v9** to see God's promise about this.

Read Luke 19v36-38 to see how the crowds reacted.

TALK

Did the people notice Jesus coming? What did they do? (Put their cloaks on the road, & shouted praises to God. Note: they also put palm branches on the road, John 12v13) Who did they say had sent Jesus as King? (God—"the Lord"v38)

PRAY

The crowds in Jerusalem praised God for sending Jesus. Do you want to thank God for that too? Why? What else can you praise God for?

BUILDING UP

XTB today looks at how the crowds welcomed Jesus on Palm Sunday as the King sent by God.

Ask your child to tell you about Jesus' arrival in Jerusalem. What happened? Why were the crowds so excited to see Jesus? What do they think the stones would have said? (v40) Are they excited that Jesus came as Rescuer? Are you? Why?

Today's passages are:
Table Talk : Luke 19v45-46
XTB : Luke 19v45-48

TABLE TALK

DO Imagine sitting at a table—and one of you suddenly tips it over! (Try it, if you can!) What would happen? Would anything get broken? How would you all feel?

READ In today's reading, Jesus drives a group of salesmen out of the Temple courtyards. The other Gospels (Matthew, Mark & John) tell us He tipped all the tables over too! **Read Luke 19v45-46**

TALK Which building did Jesus go to? What did Jesus do there? Jesus said God's Temple should be a "House of Prayer". What do you think He meant? Why was Jesus so angry? (God's Temple was being used for profit, not prayer.) Can you think of other times when it's right to be angry? What should we do then? (See Notes for Parents.)

PRAY Ask God to help you live the way He wants, even when that's hard or makes you unpopular.

BUILDING UP

Today's **XTB** notes look at why Jesus cleared the salesmen out of the Temple courtyards—and ask what we should do when we see wrong things happening. Please see Notes for Parents for suggestions on how to follow up today's XTB notes.

THE TEMPLE COURTYARDS

Old Testament law required that people made a sacrifice when they went to the Temple—often pigeons or a lamb—or gave a gift of money. (Only Temple money would do—Roman currency was not accepted.)

There was a scam going on between the priests and the salesmen, so that only birds and animals bought within the Temple courtyards were accepted as suitable for the sacrifice. This meant that the salesmen could charge excessive prices, and the people had no choice but to buy from them. This explains Jesus' reaction—"you have turned it into a hideout for thieves!" (v46, GNB)

WAS JESUS RIGHT TO BE ANGRY?

Some children (and adults!) may feel it was wrong for Jesus to drive the salesmen out in this way. It certainly doesn't fit the image of "Gentle Jesus, meek and mild"! However, Jesus' actions are consistent with the character of God shown throughout both Old and New Testament. While God is totally loving—as shown ultimately by sending His Son to die for us—God is also totally just.

There are times for us too when it is right for us to be angry. When we hear of someone being bullied, or see victims of crime on the news, it is right for us to be angry on their behalf. You may want to talk to your children about a right response when they see things happening that they know are wrong. For example, if they see a child at school being bullied—talk about what they should do, who to tell, and how they can show love (and forgiveness) to those involved.

Today's passages are:
Table Talk : Luke 22v3-5
XTB : Luke 22v1-6

TABLE TALK

RECAP—How did the crowds react to Jesus when He rode in on a donkey? (Day 2) How do you think the chief priests felt when Jesus threw people out of the Temple? (Day 3)

READ The chief priests want to kill Jesus— but He is very popular with the crowds. So, they need a way to arrest Him secretly. **Read Luke 22v3-5**

TALK Who agreed to help the chief priests get rid of Jesus? (Judas, one of the 12 disciples.) What were the chief priests going to give Judas? (Money—Mt 26v15 says 30 silver coins.) Who does v3 say was behind this wicked murder plot? (Satan.) The Bible shows us that the devil (Satan) always wants to spoil God's good plans. But God is much more powerful than the devil. As we will see, God's plans can't be spoilt.

PRAY Ask God to help you remember that He's always in control, even when it doesn't look or feel like it.

BUILDING UP

XTB today shows how God's Rescue Plan and the wicked murder plot came together at Passover time.

Ask your child to tell you about the two plans - the murder plot, and God's Rescue Plan. How do they know which plan is going to win?

Today's passages are:
Table Talk: Luke 22v10-12
XTB: Luke 22v7-13

TABLE TALK

DO Either: Lay a paper trail to follow, ending at a water jug; Or: Put a jug on the table. Ask **"Guess what this has to do with Easter"** (You may get surprising answers!)

READ Jesus sent Peter & John to get a room ready for the Passover meal, but they didn't know where to go. **Read Jesus' instructions in Luke 22v10-12**

TALK How did Peter & John know where to go? What was the room like? (Large, upstairs, furnished.) They were getting ready for the Passover meal. Ask your children what they know about Moses and the first Passover. Fill in any gaps if needed. (See Notes for Parents on the next page) **The key point is that it's a RESCUE story.**

THINK Passover is all about being rescued. Why do you think the first Easter happened at Passover time?

PRAY Yesterday, the murder plot looked like winning. Today, we see how Jesus had made all the plans beforehand. He knew **everything. He was in control.** Thank Him that He knows everything about **you** too.

BUILDING UP

Today's **XTB** notes show Jesus is in charge as He prepares to share the Passover meal with His disciples.

See Notes for Parents for ideas on how to follow up today's reading.

DAY 6 READY TO REMEMBER

Today's passages are:
Table Talk : Luke 22v19-20
XTB : Luke 22v14-20

TABLE TALK

What foods help you to remember special times? *(Birthday cake, Christmas pudding...)* What foods remind you of Easter?(Hot cross buns?) If you can, agree to eat some soon!

The Passover meal reminded people of the rescue from Egypt. It included roast lamb, bread and red wine. Jesus used the bread & wine to help His friends to be ready for His death. **Read Luke 22v19-20**

READ

What did Jesus say the bread was like? (His body) What was the wine like? (His blood) In churches today, Christians share bread & wine to remember Jesus' death. Why do you think Jesus' followers want to remember His death?

TALK

Ask God to help you never to forget that Jesus loves you so much that He died to rescue you.

PRAY

BUILDING UP

The main point of **XTB** today is that Jesus knew everything that would happen. He was always in control. Ask your child to tell you about today's story. Jesus knew everything that would happen **then,** and knows everything that happens to us **now.** (Talk about some examples.) How does that make you feel about Jesus?
Talk to Him about it.

DAY 5-6 Notes for Parents

PASSOVER

Around 1400 years before Jesus was born, the Israelites (God's chosen people) were living in Egypt. They were slaves, being cruelly treated by Pharaoh the king, so they cried out to God for help. God sent 10 plagues on the Egyptians—and chose Moses to be their leader—to rescue them from Egypt and to bring them to the land God had promised them.

Jewish people have celebrated Passover ever since—to remember how God kept His promise and rescued His people.

Why did Easter happen at Passover time?

Passover is all about being Rescued. When Jewish people celebrate the Passover meal they are remembering God's faithfulness in rescuing the Israelites from Egypt.

Ultimately, God's faithfulness in rescuing His people is seen by Him sending His only Son, Jesus, to be our Rescuer. Jesus died on the first Good Friday to save people from their sins.

You will name him Jesus—because he will save his people from their sins. *Matthew 1v21*

Christ Jesus came into the world to save sinners. *1 Timothy 1v15*

THE PASSOVER MEAL

The first ever Passover meal happened on the evening before the Israelites left Egypt. (See Exodus 12v1-14 for details.) The meal included roast lamb and unleavened bread (bread without yeast). When Jewish people celebrate Passover today, their meal still includes lamb and unleavened bread to remind them of the first Passover.

DAY 7

Today's passages are:
Table Talk : Luke 22v42-44
XTB : Luke 22v39-46

TABLE TALK

Think of something you each hate doing.
(Tidying your room, washing up, saying sorry...)
Would you rather do it straight away, put it off
until later, or not do it at all?

READ It's important to remember that Jesus
was always in control. That means He
had a choice. He didn't have to die on
the cross. He could have chosen not to.
In today's reading, Jesus is praying about His
choice. **Read Luke 22v42-44**

TALK "Father, if you are willing, take this cup
from me; yet not my will, but yours be
done." What does this prayer mean?
(Dying on the cross would be like drinking a
cup of suffering—but Jesus chooses to obey
God's will for Him.) Why do you think Jesus
chose to obey God and die for us? (See 1 John
3v16)

PRAY Give thanks to Jesus for loving us so
much He chose to die for us. Ask
God to help you to obey Him too,
even when that's hard.

BUILDING UP

XTB today compares Jesus'
choice (to obey God), with the
disciples' choice (to give in to
temptation and sleep!).

Ask your child about the difference
between Jesus' choice, and the disciples
choice. What will help your child (&
you) to choose to obey God?

DAY 8

Today's passages are:
Table Talk : Luke 22v49-51
XTB : Luke 22v47-53

TABLE TALK

Close your eyes and imagine the scene. It's
a Thursday evening—late and dark. Jesus
and His disciples are in a quiet garden at
the bottom of a hill. Jesus sees lights
coming down the hill towards Him. It's a
crowd of soldiers, carrying swords and
flaming torches. What do you think Jesus
will do?

READ Jesus could have escaped—but He
didn't! Instead He waited for the
soldiers to arrive—brought by Judas.
Read Luke 22v49-51

TALK What did Jesus' followers do?
(Fight!) What did Jesus do for the
injured servant? Why do you think the
disciples started to fight—and why did
Jesus stop them? (Refer back to yesterday,
when Jesus chose to obey His Father and
die for us.)

PRAY Jesus allowed Himself to be
arrested as part of God's Rescue
Plan. Thank Jesus for choosing to
rescue you

BUILDING UP

Today's **XTB** notes show that
Jesus chose to die to rescue us.

Ask what your child has learnt about
Jesus today. Read **The Sin Solution**
together (after page 8 of XTB).
Together, think of one sentence
to sum up why Jesus died.

DAY 9 BUBBLE TROUBLE

Today's passages are:
Table Talk : Luke 22v60-62
XTB : Luke 22v54-62

TABLE TALK

When Jesus was arrested, Peter followed. But people began to recognise him...*(If you can, split the voices between 2 or more of you.)*

Voice 1: This man was with Jesus!
Peter: I don't even know him!
Voice 2: You are one of them, too!
Peter: Man, I am not!
Voice 3: There isn't any doubt that this man was with Jesus, because he also comes from Galilee.
Peter: Man, I don't know what you're talking about!

READ **Read Luke 22v60-62** to find out what happened next.

TALK How many times did Peter deny knowing Jesus? (3) How do you think Peter felt? Why? What should we do when **we** let Jesus down? *(Talk about some examples.)*

Much later, Peter was able to say sorry, and Jesus forgave him. Ask Jesus to forgive you for letting Him down, and to help you to go on serving Him, just as Peter did.

PRAY

BUILDING UP

In today's **XTB** notes we see how Peter denied knowing Jesus—after promising that he wouldn't.

Ask your child to tell you today's story. Talk about times when they (& you) let Jesus down. Tell Jesus how you feel. Ask Him to forgive you.

DAY 10 WHO'S ON TRIAL?

Today's passages are:
Table Talk : Luke 22v67-70
XTB : Luke 22v66-71

TABLE TALK

Imagine standing outside a supermarket and asking "Who is Jesus?" What answers do you think you might get? *(A baby born at Christmas, a fairy tale, God's Son...)*

Jesus had been arrested and dragged in front of an illegal court. They wanted to know "Who is He?". Listen for **three titles** given to Jesus. **Read Luke 22v67-70**

READ

TALK What were the three titles?
(Christ/Messiah, Son of Man, Son of God) Christ isn't Jesus' surname! It means "God's chosen King". The Bible tells us that Jesus is the **Son of God** sent as our **King** to **Rescue** us. Did Jesus' enemies believe this?(v71) *(No, they think He's lying.)* What is **your** answer to "Who is Jesus?" Why do you believe this?

Ask God to help you to learn more about Jesus from the Bible.

PRAY

BUILDING UP

XTB looks at what Jesus' enemies believed about Jesus—and asks what your child believes about Him.

There are 5 statements about Jesus at the end of today's XTB notes. Ask which sentences your child ticked, and why. Discuss how you can help each other learn more about Jesus. (e.g. *read the Bible, learn memory verses, attend church regularly...*)

Today's passages are:
Table Talk : Luke 23v4+8
XTB : Luke 23v1-12

TABLE TALK

Who's the most powerful person at your school/work? In the country? In the world?

READ

Jesus' enemies sent Him to see two of the most powerful men in Jerusalem. **Pontius Pilate** was the Roman Governor. **Read Luke 23v4**

According to Pilate, what had Jesus done wrong? *(Nothing)*

Herod was the Jewish king of the north of Israel: **Read Luke 23v8**

How long had Herod been waiting to see Jesus? Why? *(to see a miracle)*

TALK

These powerful men could have freed Jesus, but they didn't! (Even though Pilate knew Jesus had done nothing wrong.) They **didn't care** who Jesus was. How can you show this Easter that you **do care** about Jesus? (Make & give cards with Bible verses inside, invite a friend to an Easter service...)

PRAY

Pray about your ideas. Ask God to help you.

BUILDING UP

The main point of **XTB** today is that God is more powerful than Pilate or Herod. God's plans always come true.

Ask your child to tell you about today's reading. Who's the most powerful person in the story? Does this help them to trust God? Why?

Today's passages are:
Table Talk: Luke 23v23-25
XTB: Luke 23v13-25

TABLE TALK

(You need pen and paper.) Play two quick games of Hangman. The first word is **PASSOVER**, the second is **RESCUE**. What's the link between these words? *(See Day 5)*

DO

Every year, the Romans set one prisoner free at Passover time. Pilate wanted to free Jesus—but Jesus' enemies were calling for a murderer called Barabbas to be freed instead.
Read Luke 23v23-25

READ

Who did Pilate set free? *(The murderer, Barabbas.)* Who did he sentence to death? *(Jesus)* Pilate knew that Jesus was innocent. He could **do the right thing**—and set Jesus free—or he could **follow the crowd**—and have Jesus killed. Which did Pilate do?

TALK

Think of times when you are tempted to follow the crowd. Ask God to help you to do the right thing instead.

PRAY

BUILDING UP

Today's **XTB** notes show that Jesus died to rescue **everyone**—not just the people who rejected and killed Him 2000 years ago, but us as well.

Ask who rejected Jesus in today's story. The XTB notes add **EVERYONE** to this list. Why do you think that is? Look up John 3v16 together. What does this say about "everyone"? ("whoever" in some Bible versions)

DAY 13 THE KING WHO CAME TO DIE

Today's passages are:
Table Talk : Luke 23v38
XTB : Luke 23v32-38

TABLE TALK

(Optional) Display three crosses—**see Notes for Parents** (Day 13). Explain that the Romans crucified Jesus with two other men. He was nailed to a cross and left to die.

It was a Roman custom to put a sign on each cross to show what that person had done wrong. The two men next to Jesus were both thieves, but Jesus had done **nothing** wrong! **Read Luke 23v38**

READ

What did Jesus' sign say? *(King of the Jews)* Add the labels **Thief, King & Thief** *to the three crosses.* Talk about the other labels—**Sinful** and **Perfect**. Which should be given to each man? Add the labels to the crosses—**see Notes for Parents.**

TALK

PRAY

If you chose a label for Jesus, what would it say? (King, Rescuer, Friend...?) Thank Jesus for being like this.

BUILDING UP

The theme of today's XTB notes is that Jesus was a King who came to die so that we could be forgiven.

Ask your child to explain the labels the Romans put on the crosses. Do they think King is a good label for Jesus? Why? Read v34 together. Can anyone be forgiven? (Even those who killed Jesus!) Why? (John 3v16)

DAY 13-14 Notes for Parents

MAKING A DISPLAY

Children often understand things better when they have something to look at. The next two days include ideas for a simple display to help them understand what happened when Jesus died. You will need:

• Three paper crosses
• Seven labels—**Thief** (X2), **King, Sinful** (X2), **Perfect** and **Believer**

Older children might like to make these labels, or design them on a PC.

On Day 13:

Display the three crosses, side by side. Put labels above them as shown —

Thief, King, Thief—as the Romans did. *(Jesus was in the middle.)*

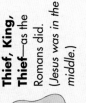

Stick the other labels on the crosses, to show what each man was like.

On Day 14:

Add **Believer** below the left-hand cross. To show what happened as Jesus was dying, swap **Perfect** from Jesus' cross, with **Sinful** from the Believer's cross. Explain that as Jesus died, He took the punishment for this man's sin. He was now forgiven, and could join Jesus in paradise, just as Jesus promised him (v43).

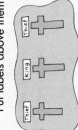

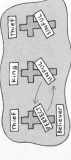

Today's passages are:
Table Talk: Luke 23v39-43
XTB: Luke 23v39-43

TABLE TALK

Recap the story from yesterday—using the display if you made it. How were the three men different? (Two were sinful, Jesus was perfect)

READ
One thief threw insults at Jesus, but the other knew that Jesus had done **nothing** wrong. **Read Luke 23v39-43**

TALK
What did the thief ask Jesus? (v42) This thief **believed** that Jesus was the King promised by God. Add **Believer to** the left-hand cross. What did Jesus promise the thief? (v43) As Jesus died, this man's sin was given to Jesus. Jesus was punished in his place. The thief was now forgiven. Swap the labels **Sinful** and **Perfect**—see **Notes for Parents.**

DO
(Optional) Read **The Sin Solution** together (after Day 8 of XTB).

PRAY
Thank Jesus for dying to rescue everyone who believes in Him.

BUILDING UP

In **XTB** we focus on the thief on the cross—who was forgiven because he **believed** in Jesus.

Ask about the differences between the two thieves. Why was only one thief forgiven? Did he have to do anything else as well as believe?(No!)

Today's passages are:
Table Talk : Luke 23v44-46
XTB : Luke 23v44-46

TABLE TALK

Talk about where and why we use curtains. (e.g. on a window, as a changing room door, in a theatre...) A curtain stops us seeing in (or out).

READ
Today's passage tells us what happened when Jesus died. It also mentions a huge curtain in the Temple. It separated the rest of the Temple from the bit in the middle—where God was said to live. Only the high priest could go in there, and only once a year! **Read Luke 23v44-46**

TALK
What happened to the sun while Jesus was on the cross? (It stopped shining!) What happened to the curtain when Jesus died? (It was torn in two.) This curtain is a picture of what sin does. It reminded people that sin separated them from God. When Jesus died, He dealt with the problem of **sin**. That's why the curtain was ripped in two—to show there is nothing to separate us from God any more.

Day 15 of **XTB** has an idea for using your curtains to help you to pray.

PRAY

BUILDING UP

Today's **XTB** notes show why Jesus' death means that nothing separates us from God any more.

Ask your child to explain why the curtain in the Temple was torn.

DAY 16 THREE REACTIONS

Today's passages are:
Table Talk: Luke 23v47-49
XTB: Luke 23v47-49

TABLE TALK

DO

Quick Quiz (based on Days 13-15):

• What sign was on Jesus' cross? (King)

• Which thief was forgiven by Jesus? (The one who believed in Jesus)

• Why was the Temple curtain torn? (To show nothing separates us from God any more)

READ

We know Jesus died as our Rescuer, but the people who saw Him die didn't know that yet. **Read Luke 23v47-49** to see their reactions.

TALK

Who went home sad? (The crowds) Who stayed to watch? (His friends) Who said Jesus was a good (or righteous) man? (The Roman Centurion) Talk about **your** reactions to Jesus' death. Can you think of reasons to be sad? happy? grateful? Add more of your own.

PRAY

Thank Jesus for the **good** thing He did for you on **Good** Friday.

BUILDING UP

Ask your child to tell you about the three reactions to Jesus' death seen in today's **XTB** notes. Why do they think each group reacted like this? The day Jesus died is called **Good** Friday. Why do you think we call it that? Talk together about your own reactions to Jesus' death.

DAY 17 DEAD AND BURIED

Today's passages are:
Table Talk : Luke 23v52-53
XTB : Luke 23v50-56

TABLE TALK

Recap: In yesterday's reading, who stayed to watch after Jesus had died? (His friends, v49.)

READ

One of Jesus' followers was a rich, powerful man from Arimathea called Joseph. (Not Mary's husband.) He asked for permission to bury Jesus. **Read Luke 23v52-53**

TALK

Who did Joseph go to see? (Pilate) What did he wrap the body in? (Linen cloth) Where was Jesus buried? (A new stone tomb.)

Jesus had told His friends beforehand what would happen to Him—but they didn't understand. (**Optional**—read Jesus' words in Luke 18v31-34.) We sometimes find it hard to understand what God says in the Bible. What can help?

PRAY

Ask God to help you to understand and believe what He says in the Bible.

BUILDING UP

XTB today looks at Jesus' burial.

Ask your child to tell you about Jesus' burial—who buried Him? How and where? How do they think Jesus' friends felt? Jesus had told them what would happen, but they didn't understand (Luke 18v31-34). What helps us to understand the Bible?

Today's passages are:
Table Talk: Luke 24v4-7
XTB: Luke 24v1-12

TABLE TALK

Set the Scene: Three women went to the tomb very early on Easter Sunday morning. They had spices to put on Jesus' body. What do you think they **expected** to find?

READ

The women expected to find Jesus' body. They didn't expect to meet two angels! **Read Luke 24v4-7**

TALK

What did the angels look like? What was their message? There was only one thing left in the tomb. Do you know what it was? Check your answer in v12.

DO

(Optional) Draw a picture of the empty tomb. Write v6 above it —"**He is not here; he has risen!**"

PRAY

Thank God for bringing Jesus back to life again on Easter Sunday.

BUILDING UP

Today's XTB notes look at how Jesus' friends reacted to the empty tomb—puzzled, scared, unbelieving and amazed.

Ask your child what the women found when they went to the tomb. What did Peter do? How did Jesus' friends react to the empty tomb was empty? Talk with your child about their reactions to the empty tomb—and yours. Do they feel puzzled, scared, don't believe, amazed or something different?

Today's passages are:
Table Talk : Luke 24v30-32
XTB : Luke 24v13-35

TABLE TALK

DO

(If possible, walk while talking — even if you just walk round the table!) Jesus had died. Now His tomb was empty—but nobody had seen Jesus. Two of His friends walked to a nearby village. What do you think they talked about? How do you think they felt?

READ

(Sit down again!) As they walked, Jesus came and joined them—but they didn't recognise Him! He showed them what the Old Testament said about Him. Then He joined them for a meal. He took some bread, thanked God, and shared it with His friends. (If possible, break a roll/slice of bread at this point.) **Read Luke 24v30-32**

TALK

When did they recognise Jesus? What happened next? (v31)

PRAY

Jesus' friends rushed back to tell the others that Jesus was alive (v33-35). Ask God to help you to tell your friends about Jesus this Easter.

BUILDING UP

Ask your child to retell the story of the walk to Emmaus in their own words. What do they think Jesus explained to His friends? (God's Rescue Plan) Who can they tell about Jesus? How can you help?

DAY 20 MEET JESUS!

Today's passages are:
Table Talk : Luke 24v38-43
XTB : Luke 24v36-45

TABLE TALK

Imagine being one of Jesus' disciples. Would you find it easy or hard to believe He was alive again? What would help you?

READ When Jesus suddenly appeared to His disciples they were terrified! They thought He was a ghost. **Read Luke 24v38-43**

TALK What did Jesus first tell His friends to do? (v39, to look at His hands and feet, and to touch Him.) They still couldn't believe it, so what did Jesus do next? (Eat some fish.) This helped Jesus' friends be sure that He really was alive again.

DO (Optional) Look up **Luke 1v1-4** to see why Luke wrote his book. Luke wrote his book to help us be sure of the **truth** about Jesus. How else can we learn more about Him? (e.g. church, Bible club, books…)

PRAY Ask God to help you learn more about Jesus this Easter.

BUILDING UP

Today's **XTB** notes show that after meeting His disciples, Jesus opened their minds to understand the Bible.
Ask your child what the answer to the code is. ("Open their minds") If we want to know Jesus better, we need His help. Ask Him to open your minds so that you know Him better and understand what the Bible says.

DAY 21 UP, UP AND AWAY!

Today's passages are:
Table Talk : Luke 24v50-53
XTB : Luke 24v50-53

TABLE TALK

A nine year old boy once asked me "When did Jesus die again?" How would you answer his question?

READ Jesus didn't die again! **Read Luke 24v50-53** to see what happened.

TALK Where did Jesus go? (To heaven—see Acts 1v9) What did the disciples do when they got back to Jerusalem? (v53) **Jesus is still alive today!** What does that mean for you? (You can pray to Him, He'll help you to understand the Bible, He is King of the world, He wants us to follow Him…)

DO (Optional) Write **"Jesus is Alive!"** on some paper. Stick it up where you'll all see it regularly.

PRAY Ask Jesus to help you to follow Him as King every day.

BUILDING UP

Ask your child what they learnt about Jesus today in **XTB**. (Jesus is alive today in heaven) What other things have they learnt about Jesus using **Easter Unscrambled?** Talk about what they will do next to find out more. (Read Dr. Luke's next book (Acts), or go on to the next issue of XTB, or follow the **What's Next** ideas on the back page or…)

Read some other stories written by Luke. Here are a few to start you off...

From Luke's Gospel

- Jesus is born Luke 2v1-7
- Shepherds visit Jesus Luke 2v8-20
- Jesus heals a lame man Luke 5v17-26
- Jesus calms a storm Luke 8v22-25
- Zacchaeus meets Jesus Luke 19v1-10

From Luke's second book—Acts

- Jesus goes to heaven Acts 1v6-11
- Jesus sends the Holy Spirit Acts 2v1-12
- Saul becomes a believer Acts 9v1-19
- Paul escapes in a basket Acts 9v23-25
- Peter's important dream Acts 10v9-16
- Peter escapes prison Acts 12v6-17
- Paul is shipwrecked Acts 27v39-44

Can you match these pictures to the stories from Acts?

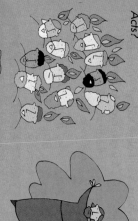

Watch out for a special edition of XTB and Table Talk for you to use on your holidays. It's called **Summer Signposts**, and it will be all about the amazing things that Jesus did and taught from John's gospel.

From the autumn of 2002 **XTB** and **Table Talk** will be available every three months to help children and families explore the Bible together.

Issue One: *The book of Beginnings*

- Explore the beginning of everything in Genesis.
- Read Matthew's biography of Jesus.
- Unscramble what it means to follow Jesus with the help of Dr. Luke's second book—Acts.

Available from Autumn 2002 from your local Christian bookshop—or call us on 020-8942-0880 to order a copy.

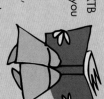